10660461

from:

imagine

written and compiled by
Barbara Paulding

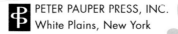

PETER PAUPER PRESS, INC.
White Plains, New York

**To good friend and painter
Karen Chapman**

Designed by David Cole Wheeler

Copyright © 2010
Peter Pauper Press, Inc.
202 Mamaroneck Avenue
White Plains, NY 10601

ISBN 978-1-59359-784-9

Printed in China
7 6 5 4 3 2

Visit us at www.peterpauper.com

INTRODUCTION

When John Lennon wrote *Imagine*, the song that became the anthem of the peace movement, he demonstrated the power of music—of imagination—to move Earth's orbit closer to peace. Being peace in the world, our hearts shine "like gold in dark times," as Clarissa Pinkola Estes writes, awakening other souls to catch fire. As world citizens spinning around the sun in a vast darkness, the choices we make shape our destiny. Radical in its energy and insight, peace is a creative act, as fierce and gentle as hard work and play, risk and love.

When the power of **LOVE**
overcomes the love of *power*
the world will know **PEACE**.

JIMI HENDRIX

Maybe we should develop
a Crayola bomb as our next
secret weapon. A happiness bomb.
A beauty bomb. And every time
a crisis developed, we would launch
one. It would explode high
in the air—explode softly—and
send thousands, millions, of little
parachutes into the air.
Floating down to earth—boxes of
Crayolas.... And people would smile
and get a little funny look on their
faces and cover the world
with imagination.

ROBERT FULGHUM

We shall find peace.
We shall hear angels.
We shall see the sky
sparkling with diamonds.

ANTON CHEKHOV

There are an awful lot of scientists today who believe that before very long we shall have unraveled all the secrets of the universe. There will be no puzzles anymore. To me it'd be really, really tragic because I think one of the most exciting things is this feeling of mystery, feeling of awe, the feeling of looking at a little live thing and being amazed by it and how it's emerged through these hundreds of years of evolution and there it is and it is perfect and why.

JANE GOODALL

Peace cannot be kept
by force.
It can only be achieved
by understanding.

ALBERT EINSTEIN

We are the life force power
of the universe, with
manual dexterity and two
cognitive minds. And we
have the power to choose,
moment by moment,
who and how we want
to be in the world.

JILL BOLTE TAYLOR

We live to commune.
We live to create.

PAUL GLASER

Everyone who's ever taken a **shower** has had an idea. It's the person who **gets out** of the shower, dries off and **does something** about it who makes a difference.

NOLAN BUSHNELL

The world is but a canvas
to the imagination.

HENRY DAVID THOREAU

Oppression involves a failure of the imagination: the failure to imagine the full humanity of other human beings.

MARGARET ATWOOD

We can never obtain peace in the world if we neglect the inner world and don't make peace with ourselves. World peace must develop out of inner peace.

THE DALAI LAMA

What is a television apparatus to man, who has only to shut his eyes to see the most inaccessible regions of the seen and the never seen, who has only to imagine in order to pierce through walls and cause all the planetary Baghdads of his dreams to rise from the dust?

SALVADOR DALÍ

To be creative means to be in love with life. You can be creative only if you love life enough that you want to enhance its beauty, you want to bring a little more music to it, a little more poetry to it, a little more dance to it.

OSHO

The Stone Age didn't end
because they ran
out of stones.

AUTHOR UNKNOWN

How hard to realize that every camp of men or beast has this glorious starry firmament for a roof! In such places standing alone on the mountaintop it is easy to realize that whatever special nests we make—leaves and moss like the marmots and birds, or tents or piled stone—we all dwell in a house of one room—the world with the firmament for its roof—and are sailing the celestial spaces without leaving any track.

JOHN MUIR

If everyone demanded **peace**
instead of another television set,
then there'd be peace.

JOHN LENNON

There are no days in life so memorable as those which vibrated to some stroke of the imagination.

F. SCOTT FITZGERALD

All works of love
are works of peace.

MOTHER TERESA

Statistically the probability of any one of us being here is so small that you would think the mere fact of existence would keep us all in a contented dazzlement of surprise.
We are alive against the stupendous odds of genetics, infinitely outnumbered by all the alternates who might, except for luck, be in our places.

LEWIS THOMAS

Poetry is an act of peace.
Peace goes into the making
of a poet as flour goes into
the making of bread.

PABLO NERUDA

Every one of us is precious
in the cosmic perspective.
If a human disagrees with
you, let him live. In a
hundred billion galaxies,
you will not find another.

CARL SAGAN

When you find peace within yourself, you become the kind of person who can live at peace with others.

PEACE PILGRIM

Above all, watch with
glittering eyes the whole world
around you because the greatest
secrets are always hidden
in the most unlikely places.
Those who don't believe in
magic will never find it.

ROALD DAHL

There is definitely enough love
and resources to go around.
I have wondered over the years
when this could be realized and
who would be the ones to do it.
Today, I am convinced more than
ever that this is the time

and that we are the ones we
have been waiting for—
generations of conscious beings
from all walks of life with the
courage, communications,
and know how to change
the world for the better.

CARLOS SANTANA

Imagination is the real and eternal world of which this vegetable universe is but a faint shadow.

WILLIAM BLAKE

If you have a bird's-eye perspective on the Earth and you look down at all the conflicts that are happening, all you see are two sides of a story where both people think they are right. So the solutions have to come from a change of heart, from softening what is rigid within us.

PEMA CHODRON

Only when there are many
people who are pools of
peace, silence, understanding,
will war disappear.

OSHO

Until he extends the circle of compassion to all living things, man will not himself find peace.

ALBERT SCHWEITZER

In India when we meet and part we often say, "Namaste," which means: I honor the place in you where the entire universe resides; I honor the place in you of love, of light, of truth, of peace. I honor the place within you where if you are in that place in you and I am in that place in me, there is only one of us.

RAM DASS

Peace is not an absence of war,
it is a virtue, a state of mind,
a disposition for benevolence,
confidence, justice.

BARUCH SPINOZA

We are blessed with technology that would be indescribable to our forefathers. We have the wherewithal, the know-it-all to feed everybody, clothe everybody, and give every human on Earth a chance. We know now what we could never

have known before—that we now
have the option for all humanity
to make it successfully on this
planet in this lifetime. Whether it
is to be Utopia or Oblivion will be
a touch-and-go relay race right up
to the final moment.

BUCKMINSTER FULLER

This will be our reply to violence: to make music more intensely, more beautifully, more devotedly than ever before.

LEONARD BERNSTEIN

Do not wait for **leaders**—
do it **alone**, person to person.

MOTHER TERESA

The first peace, which is the most important, is that which comes within the souls of people when they realize their relationship, their one-ness with the universe and all its powers, and when they realize that at the center of the universe dwells the Great Spirit, and that this center is really everywhere, it is within each of us.

BLACK ELK

*One day we must come
to see that peace is not merely
a distant goal we seek, but
that it is a means by which we
arrive at that goal. We must
pursue peaceful ends
through peaceful means.*

DR. MARTIN LUTHER KING, JR.

There is no trust more sacred than the one the world holds with children. There is no duty more important than ensuring that their rights are respected, that their welfare is protected, that their lives are free from fear and want and that they grow up in peace.

KOFI A. ANNAN,
FORMER U.N. SECRETARY GENERAL

Better than a thousand
hollow words, is one word
that brings peace.

BUDDHA

Let us plant **dates** even though those who plant them will never eat them. We must live by the *love* of what we will never see. This is the secret discipline. It is a refusal to let the creative act be dissolved away in immediate sense experience, and a stubborn commitment to the **future** of our grandchildren.

RUBEM ALVES

Peace is not something you wish for; it's something you make, something you do, something you are, and something you give away.

ROBERT FULGHUM

Peace may sound simple—
one beautiful word—but it
requires everything we have,
every quality, every strength,
every dream, every high ideal.

YEHUDI MENUHIN

If war is a necessary evil,
why not create peace as a
necessary good? Build it,
and everybody will come.

SWAMI BEYONDANANDA

I am done with great things and big things, great institutions and big success, and I am for those tiny invisible molecular moral forces that work from individual to individual, creeping through the crannies of the world like so many rootlets, or like the capillary oozing of water, yet which if you give them time, will rend the hardest monuments of man's pride.

WILLIAM JAMES

If we are peaceful, if we are happy, we can smile and blossom like a flower, and everyone in our family, our entire society, will benefit from our peace.

THICH NHAT HANH

Someday, after mastering the winds, the waves, the tides and gravity, we shall harness for God the energies of love, and then, for a second time in the history of the world, man will have discovered fire.

TEILHARD DE CHARDIN

The need is not really for more brains; the need now is for a gentler, a more tolerant people than those who won for us against the ice, the tiger, and the bear.

LOREN EISELEY

True peace is not merely
the absence of tension: it is
the presence of justice.

DR. MARTIN LUTHER KING, JR.

To map out a course of action and follow it to an end requires some of the same courage that a soldier needs. Peace has its victories, but it takes brave men and women to win them.

RALPH WALDO EMERSON

Peace is not something you must hope for in the future. Rather, it is a deepening of the present, and unless you look for it in the present you will never find it.

THOMAS MERTON

World peace is us....
We are each walking agents
of the vision of peace
we carry inside us.

KATHLEEN VANDE KIEFT

But peace does not rest in the charters and covenants alone. It lies in the hearts and minds of all people. So let us not rest all our hopes on parchment and on paper, let us strive to build peace, a desire for peace, a willingness to work for peace in the hearts and minds of all our people.

JOHN F. KENNEDY

Perhaps we cannot raise the winds. But each of us can put up the sail, so that when the wind comes we can catch it.

E. F. SCHUMACHER

No one should think that peace comes easily. Peace does not come by merely wanting it, or shouting for it, or marching down Main Street for it. Peace is built brick by brick, mortared by the stubborn effort and the total energy and imagination of able and dedicated people. And it is built in the living trust that, in the end, everyone can and will master their own destiny.

LYNDON B. JOHNSON

We must be prepared
to make heroic sacrifices for
the cause of peace that we
make ungrudgingly for the
cause of war. There is no task
that is more important or
closer to my heart.

ALBERT EINSTEIN

First keep the peace within
yourself, then you can also
bring peace to others.

THOMAS À KEMPIS

Peace is not the absence of conflict but the presence of creative alternatives for responding to conflict—alternatives to passive or aggressive responses, alternatives to violence.

DOROTHY THOMPSON

In the hearts of people today there is a deep longing for peace. When the true spirit of peace is thoroughly dominant, it becomes an inner experience with unlimited possibilities.

ALBERT SCHWEITZER

While you are proclaiming peace with your lips, be careful to have it even more fully in your heart.

ST. FRANCIS OF ASSISI

Political urgencies come and go, but it's a fair enough vocation to strike one match after another against the dark isolation, when spectacular arrogance rules the day and tries to force hope into hiding…. I'd like to speak of small wonders, and the possibility of taking heart.

BARBARA KINGSOLVER

How wonderful it is that nobody need wait a single moment before starting to improve the world.

ANNE FRANK

I like nonsense; it wakes up the brain cells. Fantasy is a necessary ingredient in living, it's a way of looking at life through the wrong end of a telescope. Which is what I do, and that enables you to laugh at life's realities.

DR. SUESS

*For behind all seen things
lies something vaster;
everything is but a path,
a portal, or a window
opening on something
more than itself.*

ANTOINE DE SAINT-EXUPÉRY

The goal toward which all history tends is peace.... This will to peace does not arise out of a cowardly desire to preserve one's life and property, but out of conviction that the fullest development of the highest powers of men can be achieved only in a world of peace.

ROBERT MAYNARD HUTCHINS

Each of us is put here in this time and this place to personally decide the future of humankind. Did you think you were put here for something less?

CHIEF ARVOL LOOKING HORSE

We who lived in concentration camps can remember the men who walked through the huts comforting others, giving away their last piece of bread. They may have been few in number, but they offer sufficient proof

that everything can be taken
from a man but one thing: the
last of human freedoms—to
choose one's attitude in any
given set of circumstances, to
choose one's own way.

VIKTOR FRANKL

Peace is always beautiful.

WALT WHITMAN

We find these joys to be self evident: That all children are created whole, endowed with innate intelligence, with dignity and wonder, worthy of respect.... We commit ourselves to peaceful ways and vow to keep from harm or neglect these, our most valuable citizens.

RAFFI

Nonviolence is not a garment
to be put on and off at will.
Its seat is in the heart, and
it must be an inseparable
part of our being.

MAHATMA GANDHI

You are here to realize your inner divinity and manifest your innate enlightenment. Foster peace in your own life and then apply the Art to all that you encounter.

MORIHEI UESHIBA

I believe that music can be an inspirational force in all our lives— that its eloquence and the depth of its meaning are all-important,... that music comes from the heart and returns to the heart— that music is forever growing—

that music can be one element
to help us build a new conception
of life in which the madness and
cruelty of wars will be replaced
by a simple understanding of the
brotherhood of man.

LEOPOLD STOKOWSKI

We will surely
get to our destination
if we join hands.

AUNG SAN SUU KYI,
*NOBEL PEACE PRIZE LAUREATE
AND PRISONER OF CONSCIENCE*

There's harmony and inner peace to be found in following a moral compass that points in the same direction regardless of fashion or trend.

TED KOPPEL

World peace begins with inner peace.
What is reflected on the outer is merely
a mirror of what is on the inner.
Trying to change the world without
working to change consciousness
is like trying to change the image
in a mirror without changing
the object that is being reflected.

CAROL HANSEN GREY

Another world is not only possible, she's on her way. Maybe many of us won't be here to greet her, but on a quiet day, if I listen very carefully, I can hear her breathing.

ARUNDHATI ROY

The good we secure for ourselves is precarious and uncertain until it is secured for all of us and incorporated into our common life.

JANE ADDAMS

Compassion is the key to a peaceful life. We can only realize our own divinity as it is reflected in the eyes of others.

IAN THRASHER

One of the most calming and powerful actions you can do to intervene in a stormy world is to stand up and show your soul. Soul on deck shines like gold in dark times. The light of the soul throws sparks, can send up flares, builds signal fires, causes proper matter to catch fire. To display the lantern of soul

in shadowy times like these—to be fierce and to show mercy toward others, both, are acts of immense bravery and greatest necessity. Struggling souls catch light from other souls who are fully lit and willing to show it. If you would help to calm the tumult, this is one of the strongest things you can do.

CLARISSA PINKOLA ESTES

Peace is a civil right which makes other human rights possible. Peace is a precondition for our existence. Peace permits our continued existence.

DENNIS KUCINICH

As I have said, the first thing
is to be honest with yourself.
You can never have an impact on
society if you have not changed
yourself.... Great peacemakers
are all people of integrity,
of honesty, but humility.

NELSON MANDELA

I think we can, really, transform the world in all sorts of ways. There could be a new movement growing up, rising from the ground, reaching for the light, and growing strong, just like a tree.

PETER GABRIEL,
MUSICIAN AND CO-FOUNDER OF WATCHDOG GROUP WITNESS AND GLOBAL THINK TANK THE ELDERS

That's all nonviolence is—
organized love.

JOAN BAEZ

Despite all of the ghastliness that is around, human beings are those that are made for goodness. The ones that are held in high regard are not the ones that are militarily powerful, nor even economically prosperous. They have a commitment to try and make the world a better place.

DESMOND TUTU

**Everything
you can imagine
is real.**

PABLO PICASSO

For building a non-violent peaceful
society in the nations of the world
constructive work is integral....
Each one nation and each citizen
will have to build it brick by brick,
by person to person.

ELA BHATT

The earth is but *one country* and mankind its citizens.

BAHA'ULLAH

Every human being has to find their own peace. Peace is within you and me. When you and I can experience who we really are, what life is, and what we are doing here, that's the day peace will begin in this world.

PREM RAWAT

We don't have to engage in grand, heroic actions to participate in the process of change. Small acts, when multiplied by millions of people, can transform the world.

HOWARD ZINN

All great deeds and
all great thoughts have a
ridiculous beginning.

ALBERT CAMUS